# PEP

C000101348

# Pastries

**KÖNEMANN**

# Pastry Basics

Good pastry is the delicious hallmark of an accomplished cook and, once you've learnt the secrets, it's surprisingly easy.

Making pastry from scratch is not difficult but it certainly *is* worthwhile, as the flavour is far superior to that of commercially prepared pastry. Shortcrust pastry is fairly quick and easy to make. Admittedly, making your own rough puff or Danish pastry takes a little time and care and is perhaps not as convenient as using frozen puff pastry for spur of the moment cooking. It does freeze well, however, so if the recipe calls for a half quantity of puff or Danish pastry, wrap the remainder tightly in plastic wrap and freeze for up to one month.

Whichever pastry you make, keeping the following points in mind will ensure success every time.

**Keep cool.** The ideal conditions for making pastry are at cool room temperature. The butter should be chilled and your hands cool when rubbing the butter into the flour. Use just your fingertips when doing this, as the palms of your hands will tend to be warm. The water should be cold or, preferably, chilled.

**Work quickly and lightly.** Overhandling pastry will make it toughen and shrink when cooked. Rub the butter in lightly and don't stir in the water: 'cut' it through with a knife. Never knead pastry (except Danish): just press it lightly together into a ball.

**Watch the moisture content.** All flours vary from brand to brand, and even batch to batch, in their moisture content. This will determine how much water you add when making pastry, which is why we don't add all the water at once. Cut the liquid through, then test by pinching a little together in your fingertips. If it holds together and doesn't crumble, you won't need more liquid. If you make the pastry too dry, it will be brittle and difficult to put into the tins, too wet and it will shrink when cooked.

**Rolling.** Turn the pastry out onto a lightly floured surface to roll. Always roll from the centre outwards, rotating the pastry, rather than backwards and forwards. If you like, you can roll the pastry on a sheet of non-stick baking paper—this is less messy than sprinkling flour about. The pastry can then be inverted into the tins and the paper peeled away. Re-use the paper when baking blind:

**Resting.** Once the pastry is made, line the tins as directed in the recipe, then refrigerate for about 15 minutes before proceeding. This allows the protein in the flour to 'relax' and reduces the shrinkage.

**Baking blind.** This prevents the bases becoming soggy if they have a moist filling. The pastry is covered with baking paper, then filled with dried beans or rice. This weighs the pastry down to prevent it rising on the base. After a time in the oven, the paper and rice is removed and the pastry base is baked a little longer. (Some small tart cases are simply pricked, then baked empty.) Cool completely before filling. If the filling has been cooked, it too must be cooled before using, once again to prevent sogginess.

## Choux Pastry

*60 g (2 oz) butter*
*1/2 cup (125 ml/4 fl oz) water*
*1/2 cup (60 g/2 oz) plain flour, sifted*
*2 eggs, lightly beaten*

1. Chop the butter and put in a pan with the water. Stir over low heat until melted, then bring to the boil.
2. Immediately remove the pan from the heat and add the flour all at once. Beat with a wooden spoon until smooth. Return to the heat and continue to beat for about 2 minutes until the mixture forms a mass, thickens and leaves the side of the pan.
3. Remove from the heat and transfer to the bowl of electric beaters; leave to cool for 5

*Beat until the mixture leaves the side of the pan.*

*Add the egg, beating until thick and glossy.*

minutes. Add the egg, a little at a time, beating well between each addition, until the mixture is thick and glossy. You may not need to add all the egg.
4. Shape the pastry onto trays and cook as directed in the recipe. If not completely dried out, return to a slow 150°C (300°F/Gas 2) oven for 5–10 minutes.

## Plain Shortcrust Pastry

*2 cups (250 g/8 oz) plain flour*
*125 g (4 oz) cold butter, chopped*
*1 egg yolk*
*3–4 tablespoons cold water*

1. Sift the flour into a large mixing bowl and add the butter. Rub the butter into the flour with your fingertips until fine and crumbly.
2. Add the combined egg yolk and 3 tablespoons of the water. Cut with a knife to form a dough, adding the remaining water if necessary. Turn onto a lightly floured surface and gather together to form a smooth dough. Cover with plastic wrap and refrigerate if not immediately required. If the weather is hot, chill for at least 30 minutes, before proceeding with the recipe as directed.

*Rub the butter into the flour with your fingertips.*

*Mix in the liquid with a knife to form a dough.*

## Food Processor Pastry

Shortcrust pastry can be made very easily in the food processor, but care must be taken not to overwork it. 'Rub' the butter into the flour by processing in short bursts, using the pulse button if you have one, until the mixture is fine and crumbly. Add most of the liquid and, again, process in short bursts until the mixture just comes together in small particles, adding more liquid if necessary.

If you continue to process until the mixture forms a ball, you will find that it is overworked and the pastry will be tough. Instead, turn the mixture out onto a lightly floured surface and press together to form a clump, before rolling out as required.

## Sweet Shortcrust Pastry

*2 cups (250 g/8 oz) plain flour*
*125 g (4 oz) cold butter, chopped*
*1/4 cup (60 g/2 oz) caster sugar*
*2 egg yolks*
*1 teaspoon vanilla essence*
*2–3 tablespoons cold water*

**1.** Sift the flour into a large mixing bowl and add the butter. Using your fingertips, rub the butter into the flour until fine and crumbly. Stir in the sugar.
**2.** Add the combined egg yolks, vanilla essence and 2 tablespoons of the water. Cut with a knife to form a dough, adding the remaining water if necessary. Turn out onto a lightly floured surface and gather together to form a smooth dough.

## Rough Puff Pastry

*90 g (3 oz) unsalted butter*
*90 g (3 oz) cooking margarine*
*2 cups (250 g/8 oz) plain flour*
*pinch of salt*
*3/4 cup (185 ml/6 fl oz) cold water*
*1 teaspoon lemon juice*

**1.** Place the butter and margarine together on a large plate. Using two knives, roughly chop the fats together, then cover and chill. When cold and hard, chop the combined fats into small cubes.
**2.** Sift the flour and salt into a large bowl. Add the cubes of fat to the flour. Using a knife, cut in the fat until just

*Stir in the liquid without breaking up the fat.*

*Fold the dough into thirds by bringing in the sides.*

*Continue rolling and turning four more times.*

coated with the flour. Combine the water and lemon juice and add most of it to the bowl. Cut into the flour with a dinner knife, without breaking up the fat. Add more of the liquid if necessary.
**3.** With floured fingers, gently bring together into a rough ball. Turn out onto a floured surface and form into a

rectangle. Do not knead. Roll the dough out into a 45 x 15 cm (18 x 6 inch) rectangle, keeping the sides and ends straight.
4. Fold the dough into three layers by folding the bottom third up and then the top third down. Seal the edges lightly with a rolling pin. Give a quarter turn clockwise: the top edge will now be to the right as if it were a book. Cover and refrigerate for 15 minutes. Repeat rolling, folding and turning clockwise four more times. Refrigerate between rollings if the dough becomes too soft. Chill for at least 30 minutes after the final rolling.
5. Roll and shape or cut the pastry as required in the recipe.

## Danish Pastry

*1/2 cup (125 ml/4 fl oz) warm milk*
*7 g (1/4 oz) sachet dried yeast*
*1 teaspoon caster sugar*
*2 cups (250 g/8 oz) plain flour*
*1/2 teaspoon salt*
*1/4 cup (60 g/2 oz) caster sugar, extra*
*1 egg, lightly beaten*
*1 teaspoon vanilla essence*
*250 g (8 oz) cold unsalted butter*

1. In a small bowl, mix together the milk, yeast and sugar. Cover and leave in a warm place for 5 minutes, or until the mixture is frothy.
2. Sift the flour into a large bowl with the salt and stir in the extra sugar. Make a well in the centre and add the yeast mixture, egg and vanilla essence all at once. Mix to a firm dough. Turn onto a floured surface and knead for 10 minutes to form a smooth, elastic dough.
3. Place the dough in a lightly greased bowl, cover and set aside in a warm place for 1 hour or until doubled in size. Meanwhile roll the cold butter between two sheets of baking paper to a 15 x 20 cm (6 x 8 inch) rectangle and then refrigerate until required.
4. Punch down the dough and knead for 1 minute. Roll out to a rectangle 25 x 30 cm (10 x 12 inches). Place the butter in the centre of the dough and fold up the bottom and top of the dough over the butter to join in the centre. Seal the edges with a rolling pin.
5. Give the dough a quarter turn clockwise then roll out to a 20 x 45 cm

(8 x 18 inch) rectangle. Fold over the top third of the pastry, then the bottom third and then give another quarter turn clockwise. Cover and refrigerate for 30 minutes. Repeat the rolling, folding and turning four more times. Wrap in plastic wrap and refrigerate for at least 2 hours before using.

*Add the yeast mixture, egg and vanilla essence.*

*Set aside for about an hour until doubled in size.*

*Fold the dough over to enclose the butter.*

# Sweet Pastries

**D**elicious treats for morning coffee or afternoon tea with friends, or perhaps for an indulgent moment on your own.

## Chocolate Eclairs

*Preparation time:*
 50 minutes
*Total cooking time:*
 25–30 minutes
*Makes 12*

1 quantity choux pastry
 (page 3)
100 g (3¹/3 oz) dark
 chocolate, chopped

**Cream Filling**
300 ml (9¹/2 fl oz)
 cream, chilled
1 tablespoon icing
 sugar
1 teaspoon Grand
 Marnier or Cointreau
1 teaspoon grated
 orange rind

**1.** Preheat the oven to moderately hot 190°C (375°F/Gas 5). Line a tray with baking paper and mark with 10 cm (4 inch) lines to use as a piping guide. Spoon the choux mixture into a piping bag fitted with a 1 cm (¹/2 inch) plain nozzle. Pipe twelve 10 cm (4 inch) fingers, a little apart, onto the tray, cutting off with a wet knife. Bake for 10 minutes, then reduce the oven to moderate 180°C (350°F/Gas 4) and bake for 15–20 minutes. Pierce, to allow steam to escape; cool on a wire rack.
**2.** Melt the chocolate in a small bowl over simmering water. Split each eclair in half and spread chocolate along the top half. Leave on a wire rack to set.
**3. To make Cream Filling:** Beat the cream, icing sugar, liqueur and rind over iced water until stiff. Spoon or pipe into the bottom half of each eclair and top with a chocolate lid. Serve immediately.

*Chocolate Eclairs*

# Baked Nectarine Tarts

*Preparation time:*
  30 minutes + resting
*Total cooking time:*
  30 minutes
*Makes 6*

1 *quantity sweet shortcrust pastry (page 4)*
1 *egg white, lightly beaten*
2 *tablespoons apricot jam*
1 *cup (250 g/8 oz) caster sugar*
2 *cups (500 ml/16 fl oz) water*
3 *small nectarines*

### Filling
90 *g (3 oz) butter*
1/2 *cup (125 g/4 oz) caster sugar*
1 *teaspoon grated lemon rind*
2 *eggs, lightly beaten*
3 *tablespoons self-raising flour, sifted*
1/2 *cup (60 g/2 oz) ground almonds*
2 *tablespoons milk*
1/2 *cup (65 g/2 1/4 oz) flaked almonds*

**1.** Grease six deep, fluted 10 cm (4 inch) loose-based tins lightly with melted butter. Roll the pastry between two sheets of baking paper and line the tins with the pastry. Prick lightly with a fork, place on a baking tray and chill for at least 20 minutes. Preheat the oven to moderate 180°C (350°F/Gas 4). Bake the pastry for 10 minutes, remove from the oven and brush the bases lightly with egg white to seal. Cool and then spread each evenly with apricot jam.
**2.** Place the sugar and water in a pan and stir for 2 minutes, or until the sugar has dissolved. Add the nectarines and simmer for 5 minutes, or until their skins have loosened. Remove from the heat and leave in the syrup for a further 10 minutes. Remove, peel, halve and stone the nectarines.
**3. To make Filling:** Cream the butter, sugar and lemon rind with electric beaters for 3 minutes, or until light and creamy. Beat in the eggs a little at a time. Using a metal spoon, fold in the flour and ground almonds, then the milk last.
**4.** Place a nectarine half, cut-side-down, into each pastry shell. Spoon the filling into the pastries and smooth the surface. Divide the flaked almonds evenly over the top. Bake for 20 minutes, or until set and golden brown. Serve warm or cold.

# Almond Cherry Danish Cushions

*Preparation time:*
  30 minutes + rising
*Total cooking time:*
  12 minutes
*Makes 12*

1/2 *quantity Danish pastry (page 5)*

### Almond Filling
30 *g (1 oz) softened butter*
4 *tablespoons caster sugar*
1/2 *cup (75 g/2 1/2 oz) finely chopped almonds*
*almond essence*
*beaten egg, to glaze*
6 *maraschino cherries*

### Almond Glacé Icing
1/2 *cup (60 g/2 oz) sifted icing sugar*
2–3 *teaspoons milk*
*few drops almond essence*

**1.** Grease two baking trays with melted butter. Roll out the dough to 24 x 32 cm (9 x 12 inches) and cut into twelve 8 cm (3 inch) squares. Mix together the butter, sugar, almonds and a few drops of almond essence to make a smooth paste.
**2.** Place a teaspoon of filling in the centre of

*Baked Nectarine Tarts (top) with Almond Cherry Danish Cushions*

each square and fold in the four corners. Secure the tips with beaten egg and push a halved cherry into the centre; put on the trays.

3. Preheat the oven to moderately hot 200°C (400°F/Gas 6). Cover the pastries loosely with plastic wrap and leave in a warm place for 20 minutes until risen. Glaze with egg.

4. Bake for 12 minutes, or until golden brown. Cool on a wire rack. Mix together the icing ingredients until smooth and drizzle over the pastries.

9

# Amaretto Mousse Tarts

*Preparation time:*
  30 minutes + chilling
*Total cooking time:*
  12 minutes
*Makes 8*

1 quantity sweet
  shortcrust pastry
  (page 4)
chocolate shavings and
  drinking chocolate
  powder, to decorate

*Filling*
1 cup (250 ml/8 fl oz)
  milk
200 g (6¹/2 oz) white
  marshmallows
3 teaspoons instant
  coffee granules
2 tablespoons Amaretto
  liqueur
1 cup (250 ml/8 fl oz)
  cream, whipped

**1.** Preheat the oven to
moderate 180°C
(350°F/Gas 4).
Divide the dough into
eight even pieces and
roll the pieces out to
line eight 10 cm
(4 inch) fluted tart tins.
Trim the edges. Prick
the bases lightly and
bake for about
12 minutes, or until
golden. Allow to cool
completely before filling.

**2. To make Filling:**
Heat the milk and
marshmallows in a pan,
stirring occasionally,
until the marshmallows
have melted. Remove
from the heat and add
the coffee granules,
stirring to dissolve. Stir
in the liqueur. Transfer
to a bowl and cool
until partially set. Fold
in the whipped cream.
**3.** Spoon into the cases,
chill until the mousse is
set, then decorate with
chocolate shavings and
drinking chocolate.

# Apple and Berry Lattice Tarts

*Preparation time:*
  30 minutes + chilling
*Total cooking time:*
  20 minutes
*Makes 8*

50 g (1²/3 oz) butter
3 tablespoons caster
  sugar
1 egg, lightly beaten
50 g (1²/3 oz) ground
  almonds
4 sheets ready-made
  puff pastry
1 cup pie or stewed
  apple, chopped
100 g (3¹/3 oz) fresh
  raspberries
caster sugar, to sprinkle

**1.** Lightly grease an
oven tray with melted
butter or oil. Cream
together the butter and
caster sugar, then beat
in half the beaten egg
(reserving the rest to
glaze) and the ground
almonds.
**2.** Cut eight 8 cm
(3 inch) fluted rounds
from two of the pastry
sheets and place on the
baking tray. Place 2
teaspoons of apple in
the centre of each
round. Divide the
raspberries between the
pastries, then top with
a tablespoon of the
almond filling. Brush
the outer edge of the
pastry with egg glaze.
**3.** Lightly flour both
sides of the remaining
two sheets of pastry.
Cut the pastry with a
lattice cutter, then cut
eight 8.5 cm (3¹/4 inch)
circles. Place the lattice
circles over the top of
the filling, pulling the
lattice apart a little to
fit. Press the edges to
seal. Use the back edge
of a knife to press the
edge of the pastry at
intervals. Refrigerate
for 20 minutes. Preheat
the oven to hot 210°C
(415°F/Gas 6–7). Glaze
pastries with the
remaining egg and
sprinkle lightly with
caster sugar. Bake for
20 minutes, or until
puffed and golden.

---

*Amaretto Mousse Tarts (top)*
*with Apple and Berry Lattice Tarts*

# Fresh Fruit Tarts

The combination of tangy fresh fruit, a creamy filling and pastry that melts in your mouth is utterly irresistible.

For each of these recipes use half a quantity of the sweet shortcrust pastry on page 4 (wrap the other half in plastic wrap and freeze until needed). Roll out the pastry and cut out 12 rounds, using a 7 cm (2³/4 inch) cutter. Line deep patty pans with the pastry rounds. Refrigerate for 10 minutes. Preheat the oven to 200°C (400°F/Gas 6). Cover each pastry shell with baking paper and fill with rice or beans. Bake for 10 minutes. Discard the paper and rice, then bake for a further 5–7 minutes, or until lightly golden. Cool completely before filling with your choice of fruit (see right). Makes 12.

## Kiwi Fruit Tarts

Using electric beaters, beat together 250 g (8 oz) cream cheese (at room temperature), 4 tablespoons icing sugar and 1 teaspoon each of grated lemon rind and juice. Pipe or spoon the mixture into pastry cases. Arrange slices of peeled kiwi fruit over the cream. Warm a jar of apple baby gel until just melted and brush liberally over the fruit.

## Strawberry Tarts

Hull 250 g (8 oz) small strawberries. Melt 50 g (1²/3 oz) dark chocolate and, using a small paint brush, coat each tart case with a thin layer of chocolate. Combine 1 cup (250 ml/8 fl oz) thickened cream, 2 tablespoons icing sugar, 1 teaspoon grated orange rind and 2 teaspoons Grand Marnier in a bowl over iced water and beat until firm peaks form. Pipe or spoon the liqueur cream into the cases and arrange the thinly sliced strawberries on top. Carefully brush warmed redcurrant jelly over the strawberries to glaze.

# Blueberry Tarts

Combine 2 tablespoons cornflour, 1 teaspoon grated lemon rind, 2 tablespoons each of lemon juice and caster sugar, $3/4$ cup (185 ml/ 6 fl oz) milk and a lightly beaten egg in a pan. Stir over low heat until the mixture boils and thickens, then cook for 1 minute longer. Cover and cool to room temperature, then whisk in 3 tablespoons cream. Spoon into tart cases and cover completely with 250 g (8 oz) fresh blueberries. Brush with warmed apple and blackcurrant baby gel.

*Tarts, from left:*
*Kiwi Fruit; Strawberry;*
*Blueberry; Morello*
*Cherry; Nectarine*

# Morello Cherry Tarts

Drain 720 g (1 lb 7 oz) jar Morello cherries, reserving $1/2$ cup (125 ml/4 fl oz) juice. Mix 2 tablespoons each of custard powder and caster sugar with $1/2$ cup (125 ml/4 fl oz) milk in a small pan and stir until smooth. Whisk in 155 ml (5 fl oz) sour cream and then bring gently to the boil, stirring constantly until the custard thickens. Boil gently for 1 minute, stir in 1 teaspoon vanilla essence, cover and cool. Combine 2 teaspoons cornflour, 1 tablespoon caster sugar and the reserved juice together in a small pan. Bring to the boil, stirring until thickened. Spoon the custard into the pastry cases, cover with the cherries then spoon over the warm glaze.

# Nectarine Tarts

Dissolve 1 cup (250 g/ 8 oz) caster sugar in 2 cups (500 ml/16 fl oz) water in a pan. Halve and poach 6 small nectarines in the mixture for 3 minutes, or until just tender; save $1/2$ cup (125 ml/ 4 fl oz) of the syrup. Drain the fruit on paper towels. Put 2 egg yolks with 1 tablespoon each of cornflour and caster sugar in a pan. Whisk in $3/4$ cup (185 ml/6 fl oz) milk and 3 tablespoons cream and bring slowly to the boil, stirring until thickened. Stir in $1/2$ teaspoon almond essence, then cover and cool. Put the reserved syrup, 2 teaspoons cornflour and 1–2 teaspoons brandy in a small pan. Spoon the crème into the pie cases, cover with a sliced nectarine half and brush with glaze.

13

# Mini Paris Brest

*Preparation time:*
  1 hour 10 minutes
*Total cooking time:*
  55 minutes
*Makes 6*

1 quantity choux pastry
  (page 3)

**Custard Filling**
1¹/4 cups (310 ml/
  10 fl oz) milk
3 egg yolks
2 tablespoons caster
  sugar
1 tablespoon plain flour
1 tablespoon custard
  powder
few drops almond
  essence, to taste

**Toffee**
1 cup (250 g/8 oz)
  caster sugar
¹/2 cup (125 ml/4 fl oz)
  water
¹/2 cup (60 g/2 oz)
  flaked almonds,
  lightly toasted

**1.** Preheat the oven to
moderately hot 190°C
(375°F/Gas 5). Draw
six 5 cm (2 inch) circles
on a sheet of baking
paper. Place the choux
pastry into a piping bag
with a 1 cm (¹/2 inch)
star nozzle. Pipe six
circles of choux onto
the paper. Bake for 10
minutes then reduce the
heat to moderate 180°C
(350°F/Gas 4). Bake for
15–20 minutes more, or
until well browned and
puffed. Pierce the sides
to allow the steam to
escape and cool on a
wire rack. Split in half.
**2. To make Custard
Filling:** Heat 1 cup of
milk to simmering point
in a pan. In a bowl,
whisk together the
remaining milk, egg
yolks, sugar, flour and
custard powder; slowly
pour on the hot milk,
whisking vigorously
until well combined.
Pour back into the pan
and stir over medium
heat until it boils and
thickens. Transfer to a
bowl, cover and cool.
Stir in the essence.
**3. To make Toffee:**
Combine the sugar and
water in a small pan,
stirring constantly over
low heat until the sugar
has dissolved. Bring to
the boil and boil
rapidly without stirring
for about 10 minutes or
until just golden. Place
the pan immediately
over another pan of hot
water to stop the toffee
from setting.
**4.** Immediately dip the
choux tops into the
toffee, decorate with a
few toasted flaked
almonds and place on a
wire rack to set. Pipe or
spoon Custard Filling
into the choux bases
and top with toffee lids.

# Petits Pithiviers

*Preparation time:*
  40 minutes + chilling
*Total cooking time:*
  15 minutes
*Makes 6*

¹/2 quantity rough puff
  pastry (page 4)
1 egg, lightly beaten

**Almond Filling**
45 g (1¹/2 oz) butter
4 tablespoons icing
  sugar
1 egg yolk
³/4 cup (70 g) ground
  almonds
few drops almond
  essence

**1. To make Filling:**
Using electric beaters,
beat the butter and
icing sugar in a bowl
until light and creamy.
Add the yolk and beat
well. Stir in ground
almonds and essence.
**2.** Preheat the oven to
hot 210°C (415°F/
Gas 6–7) and brush a
baking tray with melted
butter or oil. Roll out
pastry to 25 x 35 cm
(10 x 14 inches). Cut
out twelve 8 cm
(3 inch) circles. Divide
the almond filling
evenly between six
circles, leaving a 2 cm
(³/4 inch) border round
the edges. Brush the
border with beaten egg.

*Mini Paris Brest (top) with Petits Pithiviers*

**3.** Place the remaining pastry circles over the bases and almond filling, pressing the edges to seal. Place on a greased tray and chill for 30 minutes. With a blunt-edged knife press up the edges gently at intervals. Score the tops of the pastries into wedges and brush with beaten egg.
**4.** Bake for 10 minutes and then reduce the oven temperature to moderate 180°C (350°F/Gas 4) for 5 minutes, or until the pastries are golden.

**Note:** Pithiviers is a traditional French pastry, usually made in one large round. The name is pronounced *pit-i-vee-ay.*

15

1 Pipe six rounds of choux pastry onto the baking tray.

2 Pierce the sides with a sharp knife to allow the steam to escape.

# Mascarpone Berry Choux

*Preparation time:*
  1 hour
*Total cooking time:*
  40 minutes
*Makes 6*

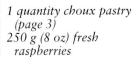

1 quantity choux pastry
  (page 3)
250 g (8 oz) fresh
  raspberries

**Raspberry Sauce**
100 g (3¹/₃ oz) frozen
  raspberries, thawed
icing sugar, to taste

**Cream Filling**
155 ml (5 fl oz) cream,
  chilled
3 tablespoons icing
  sugar, extra
3 tablespoons raspberry
  or strawberry liqueur
250 g (8 oz)
  mascarpone

1. Preheat the oven to moderately hot 190°C (375°F/Gas 5). Lightly grease a large baking tray and line with baking paper. Place the choux pastry in a piping bag with a 1.5 cm (⁵/₈ inch) star nozzle. Pipe six 4 cm (1¹/₂ inch) rounds onto the tray. Bake for 10 minutes, then reduce the oven to moderate 180°C (350°F/Gas 4) and bake for a further 15–20 minutes, or until well browned and puffed. Pierce the sides to allow steam to escape and then leave to dry out in a 150°C oven for about 10 minutes. Leave to cool completely on a wire rack and then split each choux puff in half.

2. **To make Raspberry Sauce:** Process the raspberries in a food processor until smooth. Sweeten to taste with icing sugar.

3. **To make Cream Filling:** Beat the cream and icing sugar over a bowl of iced water and then beat in the liqueur and mascarpone until just combined. Pipe or spoon Cream Filling into the bottom halves of the choux puffs. Arrange fresh raspberries over the cream and top with the lids. Sprinkle with a little extra icing sugar, if liked, and serve with Raspberry Sauce.

**Note:** Strawberries or blueberries can be used instead of raspberries.

*Mascarpone Berry Choux with Raspberry Sauce*

3 *Process the raspberries and then sweeten to taste with icing sugar.*

4 *Arrange the raspberries over the Cream Filling.*

# Cappuccino Tarts

*Preparation time:*
 40 minutes + chilling
*Total cooking time:*
 15 minutes
*Makes 6*

1¹/2 cups (185 g/6 oz)
 plain flour
3 tablespoons caster
 sugar
1 teaspoon ground
 cinnamon
125 g (4 oz) chilled
 butter, cubed
2 egg yolks
1 tablespoon iced water

**Filling**
500 ml (16 fl oz) vanilla
 ice cream
1 tablespoon instant
 coffee granules

**Topping**
2 egg whites
3 tablespoons caster
 sugar
³/4 cup (185 ml/6 fl oz)
 cream·
drinking chocolate or
 ground cinnamon,
 for sprinkling

1. Process the flour,
sugar, cinnamon and
butter in short bursts
until fine and crumbly.
Add the egg yolks and
water and process for a
further 15 seconds, or
until the mixture comes
together. Turn out onto
a floured surface and

gather the dough
together to make a
smooth ball. Preheat
the oven to moderate
180°C (350°F/Gas 4).
2. Cut the dough into
6 even pieces and roll
each out thinly to line
six 10 cm (4 inch)
fluted tart tins.
Refrigerate for 15
minutes. Prick and bake
for 12–15 minutes.
Cool, then remove from
the tins to a tray.
3. To make Filling: Let
the ice cream soften
slightly without
melting. Dissolve the
coffee in a little hot
water and stir into the
ice cream. Divide the
filling between the
cases, smooth and
freeze until firm.
4. To make Topping:
Beat the egg whites in a
clean dry bowl until
stiff, then add the sugar
gradually, beating until
thick and glossy. In a
separate small bowl,
beat the cream until
soft peaks form. Fold
the cream and egg
white mixture together
gently.
5. Spoon the topping
over the ice cream and
sprinkle with drinking
chocolate or ground
cinnamon. Freeze until
the topping is firm.
Leave the tarts to stand
at room temperature
for about 10 minutes
before serving.

# Matchsticks

*Preparation time:*
 40 minutes + chilling
*Cooking time:*
 10 minutes
*Makes 12*

1 quantity rough puff
 pastry (page 4)

**Chocolate Icing**
¹/2 cup (60 g/2 oz) icing
 sugar, sifted
1 tablespoon cocoa
 powder

**Vanilla Icing**
2 cups (250 g/8 oz)
 icing sugar, sifted
¹/2 teaspoon vanilla
 essence

**Filling**
³/4 cup (250 g/8 oz)
 raspberry jam
315 ml (10 fl oz) cream,
 whipped

1. Divide the pastry
dough in half. Roll each
half out to 30 x 20 cm
(12 x 8 inches), then cut
into twelve 10 x 5 cm
(4 x 2 inch) pieces.
2. Grease 2 oven trays
and line with baking
paper. Put the pastry on
the trays, cover and
chill for 20 minutes.
Preheat the oven to
200°C (400°F/Gas 6).
Bake for 10 minutes, or
until puffed and golden.
Cool on a wire rack.

*Cappuccino Tarts (top) with Matchsticks*

**3. To make Chocolate Icing:** Mix the icing sugar and cocoa with 1 tablespoon hot water. Spoon into a paper icing bag.

**4. To make Vanilla Icing:** In a heatproof bowl, mix the icing sugar and vanilla with 2–3 tablespoons hot water. Stand the bowl over a pan of simmering water, stirring until the icing is smooth and glossy. Spread icing over half of the pastry pieces. Pipe diagonal lines with Chocolate Icing. Drag a skewer along the icing at intervals to give a feathered effect. Leave to set on a wire rack.

**5. To make the Filling:** Spread jam and cream over the un-iced halves of the pastry and then sandwich together with the iced tops.

# Blueberry Cheesecakes

*Preparation time:*
  30 minutes + chilling
*Total cooking time:*
  35 minutes
*Makes 6*

1 quantity sweet
  shortcrust pastry
  (page 4)
155 g (5 oz) fresh
  blueberries
250 g (8 oz) cream
  cheese
1/2 cup (125 g/4 oz)
  caster sugar
1 teaspoon vanilla
  essence
1 egg
3 tablespoons cream
3 tablespoons slivered
  almonds

**1.** Preheat the oven to
moderately hot 200°C
(400°F/Gas 6). Lightly
grease six 10 cm
(4 inch) flan tins.
**2.** Divide the pastry
into six equal portions
and roll out between
non-stick paper to line
the base and sides of
the tins. Chill for 15
minutes. Bake for
15 minutes, or until
lightly browned.
Remove from the oven
and reduce the heat to
moderate 180°C
(350°F/Gas 4).
**3.** Place blueberries in
each pastry case to
cover the base. Beat the
cream cheese and sugar
together until light and
fluffy. Add the vanilla
essence and egg, mix
well and fold in the
cream. Pour over the
blueberries and sprinkle
with almonds. Bake for
20 minutes, or until the
filling has set. Dust
with icing sugar to
serve, if liked.

# Iced Palmiers

*Preparation time:*
  40 minutes + chilling
*Total cooking time:*
  15 minutes
*Makes 30*

1 quantity rough puff
  pastry (page 4)
1 egg, lightly beaten
1/2 cup (125 g/4 oz)
  caster sugar
1/2 cup (60 g/2 oz)
  ground almonds

***Almond Icing***
1 1/2 cups (185 g/6 oz)
  icing sugar, sifted
1 teaspoon butter
almond essence
1/2 cup (60 g/2 oz)
  toasted slivered
  almonds, chopped

**1.** Preheat the oven to
200°C (400°F/Gas 6).
Grease a baking tray
with melted butter or
oil. Divide the dough in
half and roll each piece
out to 30 x 20 cm
(12 x 8 inches). Brush
with beaten egg.
**2.** Combine the sugar
and almonds and
sprinkle over the
pastry; trim the edges.
Roll up one long side
halfway then roll the
other long side into the
centre to meet it. Fold
together and seal with a
little beaten egg.
**3.** Using a sharp knife,
cut 2 cm (3/4 inch)
thick slices. Place each
slice on the baking tray,
allowing room for
spreading. Flatten with
a floured spatula to
1.5 cm (5/8 inch) thick
slices. Refrigerate for
15 minutes and then
bake for 15 minutes, or
until puffed and
golden. Leave to cool
on a wire rack.
**4. To make the Almond
Icing:** Put the icing
sugar in a small bowl.
Mix the butter with
1–2 tablespoons hot
water and add to the
sugar; mix to a smooth
paste. Flavour with a
few drops of almond
essence, to taste. Spread
icing over palmiers and
sprinkle with chopped
almonds. Store in an
airtight container.

*Blueberry Cheesecakes (top)*
*with Iced Palmiers*

# Choc-Apple Pies

*Preparation time:*
  40 minutes + chilling
*Total cooking time:*
  30 minutes
*Makes 12*

1 cup (125 g/4 oz) plain
  flour
1 cup (125 g/4 oz) self-
  raising flour
1/2 teaspoon salt
1 tablespoon caster
  sugar
125 g (4 oz) chilled
  butter, chopped
100 g (3 1/3 oz) dark
  chocolate, melted and
  cooled
1 egg yolk

*Filling*
3 granny smith apples,
  peeled, cored and
  chopped
1 tablespoon water

*Topping*
90 g (3 oz) dark
  chocolate
25 g (3/4 oz) butter
2 tablespoons chopped
  walnuts

**1.** Process the flours,
salt, sugar and butter in
short bursts until fine
and crumbly. Add the
chocolate, egg yolk and
2 tablespoons cold
water and process for
15 seconds, or until the
mixture comes together.
**2.** Turn the dough onto

a floured surface and
gather together into a
smooth ball. Cover
with plastic wrap and
chill for 45 minutes.
**3.** Preheat the oven to
180°C (350°F/Gas 4).
Lightly grease a tray of
twelve 6 cm (2 1/2 inch)
patty tins. Roll two-
thirds of the pastry
thinly between two
sheets of baking paper.
Cut rounds to fit patty
tins (the pastry will be
soft and sticky).
**4. To make Filling:** Put
the apples in a pan with
the water. Cover and
simmer until puréed.
Drain away the excess
liquid and cool. Put a
heaped teaspoon of
apple filling into each
pastry shell. Roll out
the remaining pastry to
make pie tops. Moisten
the edges lightly with
water and press them
together firmly. Lightly
prick the tops of the
pies. Bake for 20
minutes; cool in the
tins for 5 minutes, then
remove to a wire rack
to cool completely.
**5. To make Topping:**
Melt the chocolate and
butter in a heatproof
bowl standing over a
pan of simmering water,
until smooth and
glossy. Spread evenly
over the pies and
sprinkle with walnuts.
Refrigerate until the
topping is set.

# Farmhouse Apple Tarts

*Preparation time:*
  20 minutes + chilling
*Total cooking time:*
  20 minutes
*Makes 6*

3 small red (gala or
  bonza) apples
1/2 quantity rough puff
  pastry (see page 4)
1 1/2 tablespoons apricot
  jam
3 tablespoons caster
  sugar
50 g (1 2/3 oz) butter,
  finely chopped
3 tablespoons apricot
  jam, extra, sieved

**1.** Lightly grease a large
oven tray. Cut the
apples in half from the
stem. Core, but leave
unpeeled. Slice as thinly
as you can, retaining
the shape.
**2.** Roll out the pastry
and trim to 25 x 36 cm
(10 x 14 inches). Cut in
half lengthways, then
across to make 6 even
rectangles. Place, well
spaced out, on the tray.
Spread each pastry
piece with a teaspoon
of apricot jam, leaving
a 2 cm (3/4 inch) border.
**3.** Divide the apple
slices evenly and
arrange along each
pastry piece, leaving a
border. Sprinkle the

*Farmhouse Apple Tarts (top) with Choc-Apple Pies*

apples with caster sugar and dot with small cubes of butter. Use the blunt side of a knife to make small indentations around the outside edge of the pastries at regular intervals. This helps them to rise and flake.
**4.** Chill for at least 20 minutes. Preheat the oven to hot 210°C (415°F/Gas 6–7) and then bake the pastries for 20 minutes, or until puffed and golden. While hot, brush lightly with warmed sieved jam to glaze. Serve warm or cold.

# Apple Turnovers

*Preparation time:*
  40 minutes + chilling
*Total cooking time:*
  25 minutes
*Makes 12*

1 quantity rough puff
  pastry (page 4)

### Apple Filling
1 cup pie or stewed
  apple
1–2 tablespoons caster
  sugar, to taste
1/4 cup (50 g/1²/3 oz)
  raisins, chopped
1/4 cup (30 g/1 oz)
  walnuts, chopped
1 egg white, lightly
  beaten
caster sugar, to sprinkle

**1.** Preheat the oven to
hot 210°C (415°F/
Gas 6–7). Grease a
baking tray with melted
butter or oil. Roll the
pastry on a lightly
floured surface to
45 x 35 cm (18 x 14
inches). Cut out twelve
10 cm (4 inch) rounds.
**2. To make Apple
Filling:** Mix together
the apple, sugar, raisins
and walnuts.
**3.** Divide the filling
between the pastry
rounds, then brush the
outer edge with water;
fold in half and pinch

firmly together to seal.
Use the back of a knife
to push up the pastry
edge at intervals. Brush
the tops with egg white
and sprinkle with caster
sugar. Make 2 small
slits in the top of each
turnover. Bake for
15 minutes, then lower
the oven temperature to
moderately hot 190°C
(375°F/Gas 5) and bake
for 10 minutes more, or
until golden.

# Currant Scrolls

*Preparation time:*
  30 minutes + rising
*Total cooking time:*
  12 minutes
*Makes 10*

1/2 quantity Danish
  pastry (page 5)

### Filling
50 g (1²/3 oz) butter,
  softened
3 tablespoons caster
  sugar
1 teaspoon ground
  cinnamon
1/2 cup (90 g/3 oz)
  currants
2 teaspoons rum
beaten egg, to glaze

### Glacé Icing
1/2 cup (60 g/2 oz) icing
  sugar, sifted
2–3 teaspoons milk

**1. To make Filling:**
In a small bowl mix
together the butter,
sugar and cinnamon.
Put the currants to soak
in the rum. Grease two
baking trays with
melted butter. Roll the
pastry out and trim to
make a 30 x 20 cm
(12 x 8 inch) rectangle.
Spread the butter and
sugar mixture over the
pastry, using a spatula
to cover the surface
evenly. Sprinkle the
currants evenly over
this and then roll up
the pastry from the
short side as if it were a
swiss roll.
**2.** Cut the roll into ten
2 cm (³/4 inch) slices.
Flatten the slices evenly
to 1¹/2 cm (⁵/8 inch)
thick with floured
hands and put on the
trays. Cover the
pastries loosely with
plastic wrap and leave
in a warm place for
20 minutes, or until
they are well risen.
Preheat the oven to
moderately hot 200°C
(400°F/Gas 6). Glaze
the pastries with the
beaten egg and then
bake for 12 minutes, or
until golden brown and
crisp. Leave to cool on
a wire rack.
**3. To make Glacé Icing:**
Mix together the icing
sugar and milk until
smooth, then drizzle
over the pastries.

*Apple Turnovers (top) with Currant Scrolls*

# Baklava

*Preparation time:*
  30 minutes
*Cooking time:*
  45 minutes
*Serves 4–6*

375 g (12 oz) walnuts,
  finely chopped
155 g (5 oz) almonds,
  finely chopped
1/2 teaspoon ground
  cinnamon
1/2 teaspoon ground
  mixed spice
1 tablespoon caster
  sugar
16 sheets filo pastry
60 g (2 oz) butter,
  melted
3 tablespoons olive oil

*Syrup*
1 cup (250 g/8 oz)
  sugar
3/4 cup (185 ml/6 fl oz)
  water
3 whole cloves
3 teaspoons lemon juice

1. Preheat the oven to
moderate 180°C
(350°F/Gas 4). Brush
the sides and base of an
18 x 28 cm (7 x 11
inch) ovenproof dish
with melted butter or
oil. Combine the
walnuts, almonds,
spices and sugar in a
bowl and divide into
three portions. Place
one sheet of pastry onto
the work surface. Brush

half the sheet with the
combined butter and oil
and fold in half
widthways. Place in
the base of the dish,
trimming the edges to
fit. Repeat with another
three sheets of pastry to
cover the base.
2. Sprinkle one portion
of walnut mixture over
the pastry. Repeat the
pastry process with
four more sheets.
Sprinkle with the
second portion of
walnut mixture.
Continue with another
four sheets of pastry,
the remaining walnut
mixture and finally the
last four sheets of
pastry. Trim the edges.
3. Brush the top of the
pastry with the
remaining butter and
oil mixture. Score the
top evenly into squares
or diamonds. Bake for
30 minutes, or until
golden and crisp.
4. To make the Syrup:
Put the sugar, water,
cloves and lemon juice
in a small pan. Stir
constantly over low
heat until the mixture
boils and the sugar has
dissolved. Reduce the
heat and leave to
simmer, without
stirring, for 10 minutes.
Cool, remove the cloves
and pour over the hot
slice. When cold, cut
into squares or
diamonds to serve.

# Cream Horns

*Preparation time:*
  40 minutes + chilling
*Total cooking time:*
  20 minutes
*Makes 15*

1/2 quantity rough puff
  pastry (page 4)
apricot jam
3 tablespoons finely
  chopped pistachio
  nuts
icing sugar, to dust

**Chantilly Cream**
315 ml (10 fl oz) cream
2 tablespoons icing
  sugar
1 teaspoon vanilla
  essence

1. Grease an oven tray
and cream horn moulds
with oil. Roll out the
pastry on a lightly
floured surface into a
30 cm (12 inch) square
and trim the edges. Cut
into fifteen strips, each
2 cm (3/4 inch) wide.
2. Moisten one long
edge with water.
Starting at the tip, wind
the pastry around the
mould, overlapping the
moistened edge. Repeat
with the remaining
pastry. Put on the tray,
cover and refrigerate
for 15 minutes. Preheat
the oven to moderately
hot 200°C (400°F/
Gas 6–7).

*Baklava (top) with Cream Horns*

**3.** Bake the pastries for 15 minutes and then remove the moulds; Reduce the oven to 180°C (355°F/Gas 4) and bake the pastries for a further 5 minutes, or until golden. Cool on a wire rack.

**4. To make the Chantilly Cream:** Beat the cream, icing sugar and vanilla essence until stiff peaks form.

**5.** To serve, spoon a little jam into the tip of each pastry horn. Pipe in the cream and sprinkle with pistachio nuts. Dust the cones with sifted icing sugar.

1 Soak the apricots in boiling water until they have softened.

2 Toss the sliced apple with the sugar, lemon juice and spices.

# Apple and Apricot Strudel

*Preparation time:*
  30 minutes + soaking
*Total cooking time:*
  40 minutes
*Makes 1 large strudel*

20 dried apricots
2 large cooking apples
3 tablespoons caster
  sugar
1 tablespoon lemon
  juice
$^{1}/_{2}$ teaspoon ground
  cinnamon
$^{1}/_{2}$ teaspoon mixed
  spice
8 sheets filo pastry
60 g (2 oz) butter,
  melted
2 tablespoons oil
1 cup (80 g/2$^{2}/_{3}$ oz)
  fresh breadcrumbs
3 tablespoons ground
  almonds
icing sugar, to dust

1. Preheat the oven to moderate 180°C (350°F/Gas 4). Lightly grease a baking tray with melted butter. Soak the apricots in boiling water for 15 minutes, or until softened; drain well.
2. Peel, core and thinly slice the apples. Place in a large bowl and add the sugar, lemon juice, cinnamon and mixed spice. Toss well with clean hands to thoroughly coat the apples. Stir in the apricots; set aside while preparing the pastry.
3. Brush a sheet of pastry with the combined melted butter and oil. Form a large rectangle by placing a second sheet halfway down the first. In a bowl, mix together the breadcrumbs and almonds and sprinkle a little over the pastry. Layer another two sheets over the top, brushing with melted butter and oil and sprinkling with breadcrumbs and almonds. Continue layering with the remaining pastry.
4. Drain the fruit filling and then spread along one long edge of the pastry, leaving a 2.5 cm (1 inch) border. Roll up the pastry, tucking in the ends to enclose the filling. Place, seam-side-down, on the tray and brush the top with melted butter. Bake for 35–40 minutes, or until golden brown and crisp. Dust with icing sugar. Serve warm or cold and cut diagonally into individual slices.

*Apple and Apricot Strudel*

*3 Layer the pastry sheets, placing a sheet halfway down to form a large rectangle.*

*4 Roll up the pastry, tucking in the ends, to enclose the filling.*

# Fig and Pear Tarts

*Preparation time:*
  30 minutes + chilling
*Total cooking time:*
  40 minutes
*Makes 6*

1¹/4 cups (155 g/5 oz)
  plain flour
¹/2 cup ground
  hazelnuts
¹/4 teaspoon salt
3 tablespoons caster
  sugar
100 g (3¹/3 oz) chilled
  butter, chopped
1 egg yolk
1 tablespoon iced water
3 tablespoons chopped
  hazelnuts

**Filling**
50 g (1²/3 oz) butter
¹/2 cup (90 g/3 oz) soft
  brown sugar
¹/2 cup (125 ml/4 fl oz)
  apple juice
2 tablespoons brandy
1 ripe pear, peeled
  and cored
250 g (8 oz) soft
  dessert figs, chopped

**1.** Put the flour, hazelnuts, salt, sugar and butter in a food processor and process in short bursts for 20 seconds, or until fine and crumbly. Add the egg yolk and water and process for a further 15 seconds, or until the mixture comes together. Turn the dough out onto a lightly floured surface and gather together to form a smooth ball. Cover in plastic wrap and put in the refrigerator for 45 minutes.
**2.** Preheat the oven to hot 210°C (415°F/ Gas 6–7). Divide the pastry into 6 pieces and roll out on a lightly floured surface to line six 6 cm individual flan tins with removable bases. Prick the pastry lightly. Bake for 12 minutes, or until cooked but only lightly coloured. Leave the tart cases to cool completely.
**3. To make the Filling:** Place the butter, sugar, apple juice and brandy in a pan and bring to the boil while stirring. Simmer until reduced and syrupy. Chop the pear into 1 cm (¹/2 inch) pieces and add to the syrup with the figs.
**4.** Place the tart cases on a baking tray and add the hot filling. Sprinkle with hazelnuts and bake for 12–15 minutes. Serve immediately with cream or ice cream.

**Note:** Soft dessert figs are dried figs that have been tenderised. They are readily available in supermarkets.

# Coconut Tartlets

*Preparation time:*
  45 minutes + chilling
*Total cooking time:*
  30 minutes
*Makes 24*

1¹/2 cups (185 g/6 oz)
  plain flour
3 tablespoons icing
  sugar
125 g (4 oz) butter,
  chopped
grated rind of 2 lemons
1 egg yolk

**Filling**
³/4 cup (175 g/5²/3 oz)
  caster sugar
3 tablespoons
  lemon juice
3 cups (300 g/9²/3 oz)
  desiccated coconut
3 eggs, lightly beaten
60 g (2 oz) butter,
  melted
3 tablespoons milk
1 teaspoon baking
  powder
3 tablespoons
  raspberry jam

**1.** Sift the flour and icing sugar into a bowl. Rub in the butter until fine and crumbly. Stir in the lemon rind.
**2.** Add the egg yolk and 3 tablespoons cold water. Mix with a knife to form a rough dough; add another tablespoon of water if necessary. Turn out onto a lightly

*Fig and Pear Tart (top) with Coconut Tartlets*

floured surface; gather together into a ball. Wrap in plastic wrap; chill for 20 minutes.
**3.** Roll the pastry out between 2 sheets of baking paper until 3 mm ($1/8$ inch) thick. Cut into 24 rounds of 7 cm ($2^{3}/4$ inches) and put in greased shallow patty tins. Cover with plastic wrap and chill for 20 minutes. Preheat the oven to 180°C (350°F/Gas 4).
**4. To make Filling:** Heat sugar and juice in a pan with $1/2$ cup (125 ml/ 4 fl oz) water until the sugar dissolves. Remove from the heat, add the coconut, eggs, butter, milk and baking powder and mix well.
**5.** Put $1/2$ teaspoon jam in each pastry, spoon the filling on top and bake for 25 minutes, or until firm and golden.

31

1 Process the dough until it just comes together. Overmixing will make it tough.

2 Lightly prick the pastry cases before baking until golden.

# Sour Cherry Tarts

*Preparation time:*
*25 minutes + chilling*
*Total cooking time:*
*15 minutes*
*Makes 6*

100 g (3¹/₃ oz) ground
  almonds
1 cup (125 g/4 oz) plain
  flour
30 g (1 oz) icing sugar
90 g (3 oz) chilled
  butter, chopped

**Filling**
250 g (8 oz) light cream
  cheese
3 tablespoons cream
1 tablespoon icing
  sugar, sifted
¹/₂ teaspoon finely
  grated lemon rind
720 g jar pitted sour
  cherries, well drained
¹/₂ cup (170 g/5¹/₂ oz)
  redcurrant jelly

1. Process the almonds, flour, icing sugar and butter in short bursts for 20 seconds, or until fine and crumbly. Add 1 tablespoon ice-cold water and process for a further 15 seconds, or until the mixture comes together. Turn the dough onto a lightly floured surface and gather together into a smooth ball. Cover with plastic wrap and refrigerate for at least 45 minutes.

2. Preheat the oven to moderate 180°C (350°F/Gas 4). Divide the pastry into six even portions and roll each out thinly, on a board sprinkled with flour, to line six 9 cm fluted tart tins. Prick the bases lightly and bake for 10 minutes, or until golden. Remove the pastry cases from the tins and leave to cool completely.

3. **To make the Filling:** Place the cream cheese in a small bowl and stir until smooth. Stir in the cream, icing sugar and lemon rind. Divide the filling between the pastry cases, spreading the surface until smooth. Arrange the cherries over the filling.

4. Gently heat the redcurrant jelly in a small pan until melted, then brush over the cherries. Refrigerate until ready to serve.

**Notes:** Bottled sour cherries are often labelled 'morello' cherries. The ground almonds add a delicious flavour to this pastry but make it a little crumbly to work with, so take extra care. Cream cheese is easier to work with if it is at room temperature.

*Sour Cherry Tarts*

*3 Fill the cooled pastry cases with the cream cheese mixture and then smooth.*

*4 Brush the melted redcurrant jelly over the cherries to glaze.*

# Pecan Coffee Tarts

*Preparation time:*
 15 minutes + chilling
*Total cooking time:*
 40 minutes
*Makes 6*

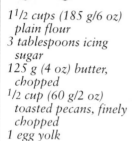

1¹/2 cups (185 g/6 oz)
 plain flour
3 tablespoons icing
 sugar
125 g (4 oz) butter,
 chopped
¹/2 cup (60 g/2 oz)
 toasted pecans, finely
 chopped
1 egg yolk

**Filling**
125 g (4 oz) unsalted
 butter
¹/2 cup (90 g/3 oz) soft
 brown sugar, firmly
 packed
4 tablespoons cream
3 tablespoons plain
 flour
2 teaspoons instant
 coffee
2 teaspoons hot water
1–2 tablespoons Kahlua
¹/3 cup (40 g/1¹/3 oz)
 pecans, coarsely
 chopped
1 tablespoon demerara
 sugar

**1.** Sift the flour and
icing sugar into a large
bowl and rub in the
butter. Stir through the
pecans, then add the
egg yolk and a little
water, if necessary, to
make the ingredients
come together and form
a dough. Cover with
plastic wrap and
refrigerate for
30 minutes. Preheat the
oven to moderately hot
200°C (400°F/Gas 6).
**2.** Divide the dough
into six equal portions.
Press each portion into
a 10 cm (4 inch) tart
tin. Prick the bases well
with a fork. Place on an
oven tray and bake for
12–15 minutes; leave to
cool. Reduce the oven
temperature to
moderate 180°C
(350°F/Gas 4).
**3. To make the Filling:**
Melt the butter and
sugar in a pan, stir until
the sugar has dissolved,
bring to the boil and
simmer gently for
5 minutes, stirring
occasionally. Remove
from the heat and beat
in the blended cream
and flour with a wire
whisk. Return to the
heat, bring to the boil
and then stir over the
heat for 3 minutes.
Remove from the heat
and add the coffee
dissolved in the water
and the Kahlua.
**4.** Pour the filling into
the pastry cases,
sprinkle with pecans
and sugar and bake for
10 minutes. Cool
slightly before serving.
Delicious with
strawberries and cream.

# Semolina Rolls

*Preparation time:*
 30 minutes
*Total cooking time:*
 35 minutes
*Makes about 20*

1 cup milk
¹/2 cup (125 ml/4 fl oz)
 cream
¹/2 cup (60 g/2 oz) fine
 semolina
4 tablespoons caster
 sugar
2 eggs, lightly beaten
2 teaspoons grated
 lemon rind
1 teaspoon vanilla
 essence
10 sheets filo pastry
60 g (2 oz) unsalted
 butter, melted
3 tablespoons icing
 sugar, to dust
1 teaspoon cinnamon,
 to dust

**1.** Preheat the oven to
moderately hot 190°C
(375°F/Gas 5) and
lightly grease an oven
tray. Put the milk,
cream, semolina, caster
sugar, eggs and lemon
rind in a heavy-based
pan and whisk together
until well combined.
Whisk over low heat
for 10 minutes, or until
thick and paste-like.
Remove from the heat
and stir in the vanilla
essence. Transfer to a
bowl, cover the surface

*Pecan Coffee Tarts (top) with Semolina Rolls*

with plastic wrap and leave to cool.

**2.** Lightly brush a sheet of filo with melted butter; put a second sheet on top and brush with butter. Cut into 4 strips widthways. Place a heaped tablespoon of filling at the base of each strip and roll up, folding in the sides of the pastry. Brush with butter and put on the tray. Repeat with rest of the filo and filling.

**3.** Bake for 25 minutes, or until puffed and golden. Dust with the combined icing sugar and cinnamon.

35

1  Remove the custard from the heat and stir in the apricot purée.

2  Make cuts into the centre from each corner of the square.

# Apricot Danish Stars

*Preparation time:*
*35 minutes + rising*
*Total cooking time:*
*25–30 minutes*
*Makes 12*

10 dried apricots
1 tablespoon caster
    sugar
1 tablespoon cornflour
1 egg yolk
1/2 cup (125 ml/4 fl oz)
    milk
1 teaspoon Grand
    Marnier or Cointreau
1/2 quantity Danish
    pastry (page 5)
beaten egg, to glaze
3 tablespoons
    apricot jam
icing sugar, to dust

**1.** Put the apricots in a pan, cover with water and simmer for 10 minutes until soft. Drain, then purée and set aside to cool. In a small pan, combine the sugar and cornflour until smooth; gradually whisk in the combined egg yolk and milk. Whisk over low heat until the mixture boils and thickens. Remove from the heat and stir in the apricot purée and liqueur. Transfer to a bowl, cover with plastic wrap and refrigerate.
**2.** Grease two baking trays with melted butter. Roll out the dough and then trim the edges to make an even 24 x 32 cm (9 x 12 inch) rectangle and cut twelve 8 cm (3 inch) squares. Make diagonal cuts from each corner to within 1 cm (1/2 inch) of the centre.
**3.** Place a heaped teaspoon of filling in the centre of each square. Fold one corner of each cut section into the centre; secure with beaten egg. Put on the trays. Cover the pastries loosely with plastic wrap and leave in a warm place for 20 minutes, or until well risen. Preheat the oven to moderately hot 200°C (400°F/Gas 6).
**4.** Glaze the pastries with beaten egg and spoon a little jam into the centre of each. Bake for 12 minutes, or until golden and crisp. Leave pastries to cool on a wire rack and then dust lightly with icing sugar to serve.

*Apricot Danish Stars*

3 Fold one corner of each cut section into the centre.

4 Glaze the pastries with beaten egg and then top with a little jam.

## Spicy Date and Hazelnut Pillows

*Preparation time:*
  *30 minutes +*
  *30 minutes chilling*
*Total cooking time:*
  *30 minutes*
*Makes about 24*

*45 g (1¹/₂ oz) butter*
*¹/₃ cup (45 g/1¹/₂ oz)*
  *soft brown sugar,*
  *firmly packed*
*¹/₂ cup (185 g/6 oz)*
  *golden syrup*
*2¹/₂ cups (315 g/10 oz)*
  *plain flour*
*3 tablespoons self-*
  *raising flour*
*¹/₄ teaspoon ground*
  *cloves*
*¹/₂ teaspoon mixed*
  *spice*
*¹/₂ teaspoon ground*
  *cinnamon*
*1 egg, lightly beaten*

### Date and
  Hazelnut Filling
*315 g (10 oz) pitted*
  *dates, chopped*
*¹/₂ cup (125 ml/4 fl oz)*
  *water*
*³/₄ cup (90 g/3 oz)*
  *roasted hazelnuts,*
  *finely chopped*
*¹/₂ teaspoon mixed*
  *spice*
*1 teaspoon grated*
  *orange rind*
*1 egg, beaten, for*
  *glazing*
*1 tablespoon demerara*
  *or raw sugar*

**1.** Put the butter, sugar and syrup in a pan; stir over low heat until dissolved, then cool for 10 minutes. Sift the flours and spices into a large bowl, add the egg and the butter mixture and stir with a wooden spoon until a sticky dough forms. Turn out onto a floured surface and knead gently until the dough loses its stickiness. Cover with plastic wrap and chill for 30 minutes.

**2. To make Filling:** Put the dates and water in a pan, bring to the boil, reduce the heat and simmer, uncovered, for 10 minutes, stirring occasionally, until thickened. Cool. Stir in the hazelnuts, mixed spice and rind. Preheat the oven to 200°C (400°F/Gas 6). Lightly grease an oven tray.

**3.** Divide the dough into four portions. Roll one portion out on a lightly floured surface into a strip about 10 cm (4 inches) wide and 20 cm (8 inches) long. Spoon a quarter of the filling like a long sausage along the centre of the strip. Brush one side with beaten egg and roll up tightly to enclose the filling: have the seam side down and press gently to seal. Put on the oven tray.

**4.** Cut the roll into shorter pillows, without cutting right through to the base. Repeat with the rest of the dough and filling and put on the oven tray.

**5.** Brush with the remaining egg, sprinkle with sugar and bake for 10–12 minutes, or until lightly browned. Cut the pillows right through to the base while hot. Leave for 5 minutes, then put on a wire rack to cool.

## Figs in Filo

*Preparation time:*
  *20 minutes*
*Total cooking time:*
  *15 minutes*
*Makes 6*

*¹/₃ cup (40 g/1¹/₃ oz)*
  *chopped walnuts*
*1 tablespoon honey*
*¹/₂ teaspoon finely*
  *grated lemon rind*
*12 sheets filo pastry*
*50 g (1²/₃ oz) butter,*
  *melted*
*6 firm ripe figs*

**1.** Preheat the oven to 180°C (350°F/Gas 4). Spread the walnuts on a tray and bake for about 3 minutes, until lightly toasted; cool. Mix with the honey and rind.

**2.** Brush a sheet of pastry with melted

*Spicy Date and Hazelnut Pillows (top) with Figs in Filo*

butter. Top with another sheet, brush with butter and repeat twice more. Cut into two rectangles. Repeat with the remaining sheets of pastry.

**3.** Trim the stalks from the figs and cut in half from the top, almost to the base. Fill with the walnut mixture. Put each fig on a pastry piece and gather up the pastry around it. Tie with string, brush with melted butter and put on a baking tray. Bake for 8–10 minutes, or until golden. Remove the string to serve.

## Pumpkin Pillows

*Preparation time:*
30 minutes
*Total cooking time:*
10 minutes
*Makes 12*

185 g (6 oz) butternut
  pumpkin, grated
1/2 cup (100 g/3 1/3 oz)
  ground almonds
3 tablespoons caster
  sugar
1/2 teaspoon ground
  cardamom
1/3 cup (50 g/1 2/3 oz)
  blanched almonds,
  toasted and chopped
6 sheets filo pastry
60 g (2 oz) ghee or
  clarified butter, melted

1. Preheat the oven to
200°C (400°F/Gas 6).
Combine the pumpkin,
ground almonds, sugar
and cardamom. Add
the chopped almonds,
reserving 1 tablespoon.
2. Brush one sheet of
pastry with ghee, top
with another and brush
with ghee. Cut into
four strips. Put 1
tablespoon of filling at
the end of each strip,
fold in the sides, brush
with ghee and roll up
into a parcel. Repeat
with rest of pastry.
3. Put the parcels on a
greased oven tray,

brush with remaining
ghee and sprinkle with
almonds. Bake for 8–10
minutes, until golden.

## Peachy Ricotta Tarts

*Preparation time:*
35 minutes + chilling
*Total cooking time:*
25 minutes
*Makes 6*

1 1/4 cups (155 g/5 oz)
  plain flour
1/4 teaspoon salt
90 g (3 oz) chilled
  butter, chopped
2 tablespoons caster
  sugar
1/2 teaspoon vanilla
  essence
1 egg yolk

*Filling*
375 g (12 oz) ricotta
1 tablespoon honey
1 egg, beaten
vanilla essence, to taste

*Topping*
425 g (13 1/2 oz) canned
  peach slices in natural
  syrup, well drained
1/2 cup (90 g/3 oz) soft
  brown sugar
30 g (1 oz) butter
1/2 cup (125 ml/4 fl oz)
  cream
1 tablespoon Grand
  Marnier liqueur

1. Process the flour,
salt, butter and sugar in
short bursts until fine
and crumbly. Add the
vanilla essence, egg
yolk and 1 tablespoon
iced water and process
until the mixture comes
together. Wrap in
plastic and chill for
30 minutes. Preheat
the oven to 180°C
(350°F/Gas 4).
2. Divide the dough
into six equal portions.
Roll each portion out
thinly to line a 10 cm
(4 inch) individual flan
tin with a removable
base. Prick the pastry
lightly and bake for
8 minutes.
3. **To make Filling:** Mix
the ingredients together
well. Quickly divide
among the hot tart
cases, spreading until
smooth. Bake for a
further 18 minutes, or
until the filling is set
and pastry cooked.
Cool completely.
4. **To make Topping:**
Cut the peaches into
thinner slices and
arrange on top of the
cold tarts. Combine the
sugar, butter, cream and
liqueur in a small pan
and bring to the boil
while stirring. Heat
until reduced and quite
syrupy, stirring
occasionally. Cool for a
few minutes until
slightly thickened, then
brush over the tarts.

*Pumpkin Pillows (top) with a Peachy Ricotta Tart*

# Fruit and Almond Filo Tarts

*Preparation time:*
  30 minutes
*Total cooking time:*
  15 minutes
*Makes 24*

12 sheets filo pastry
60 g (2 oz) unsalted
  butter, melted
100 g (3¹/3 oz) almond
  paste

### Fruit Mince
30 g (1 oz) butter
4 prunes, finely
  chopped
¹/3 cup (50 g/1²/3 oz)
  currants
¹/4 cup (30 g/1 oz)
  sultanas
¹/4 cup (50 g/1²/3 oz)
  chopped raisins
1 tablespoon mixed
  peel
2 tablespoons caster
  sugar
2 teaspoons brandy or
  rum
¹/2 teaspoon cinnamon
¹/2 teaspoon nutmeg

**1.** Preheat the oven to
moderate 180°C
(350°F/Gas 4). Very
lightly grease two
12-hole patty tins with
melted butter.
**2. To make Fruit
Mince:** Melt the butter
in a small pan, add the
remaining ingredients
and stir well to

combine. Stir over low
heat for 2 minutes, until
fruit is coated and
sugar dissolved. Cool.
**3.** Cover the filo pastry
with a slightly damp tea
towel. Cut 8 sheets into
7 cm (2³/4 inch)
squares, cover and set
aside. Cut 4 sheets into
8 cm (3 inch) squares,
cover and set aside.
**4.** Work with the
smaller squares first to
make the tart bases.
You will need 8 squares
per tart. Butter 1 square
and put another on top.
Butter and pair 6 more
squares, then arrange in
the tin as an 8-pointed
star. Continue until all
24 cases are filled.
**5.** Work with the larger
squares for the filling.
You will need 2 squares
buttered together for
each tart. Place a ¹/2
teaspoonful of almond
paste into the centre of
the square. Place a
rounded teaspoonful of
the Fruit Mince on top.
Wrap the pastry around
the filling and seal with
a little butter. Place,
seam-side-down, into
the centre of a tart case
and butter top lightly.
Repeat with remaining
filling and pastry until
all 24 tarts are filled.
**6.** Bake for 12 minutes,
or until the pastries are
crisp and golden. Serve
warm, dusted with icing
sugar, if you like.

# Sugar and Spice Palmiers

*Preparation time:*
  40 minutes + chilling
*Total cooking time:*
  15 minutes
*Makes 36*

1 quantity rough puff
  pastry (page 4)
1 egg, lightly beaten
demerara sugar, to dust

### Filling
¹/2 cup (125 g/4 oz)
  caster sugar
2 tablespoons lightly
  toasted sesame seeds
1 teaspoon ground
  cinnamon
¹/2 teaspoon ground
  ginger
¹/4 teaspoon ground
  nutmeg
¹/4 teaspoon ground
  cloves

**1.** Preheat the oven to
hot 220°C (425°F/
Gas 7). Grease a baking
tray with melted butter
or oil. Divide the dough
in half and roll each
piece out to 36 x 16 cm
(14 x 6 inches). Brush
with beaten egg.
**2. To make Filling:** Mix
together the sugar, seeds
and spices and sprinkle
evenly over the pastry.
**3.** Roll up one long side
halfway then roll the
other long side into the
centre to meet it. Fold

*Fruit and Almond Filo Tarts (top) with Sugar and Spice Palmiers*

together and seal with egg. Repeat with the other roll. Using a sharp knife, cut the rolls into 2 cm (³/4 inch) thick slices. Place each slice on the baking tray, allowing room to spread. Flatten to 1.5 cm (⁵/8 inch) with a floured spatula. Sprinkle each palmier with demerara sugar and refrigerate for 15 minutes. Bake for 15 minutes, or until puffed and golden. Cool on a wire rack.

43

# Savoury Pastries

Almost any savoury filling you care to imagine tastes even better encased in a crisp shell of freshly baked pastry.

## Cocktail Tartlet Trio

*Preparation time:*
30 minutes + chilling
*Total cooking time:*
8–9 minutes
*Makes approximately*
30 tartlet cases

1¹/2 cups (185 g/6 oz)
plain flour
¹/4 teaspoon salt
¹/4 cup (30 g/1 oz)
freshly grated
Parmesan cheese
100 g (3¹/3 oz) chilled
butter, chopped
1 egg, lightly beaten
1 tablespoon iced water

### Fillings
pesto, sun-dried
tomato, black olives;
tapenade, hard-boiled
quail eggs, flat-leaf
parsley;
light cream cheese,
chives, smoked
salmon, Lebanese
cucumber

1. Place the flour, salt, Parmesan and butter in a food processor. Process in short bursts for 20 seconds, or until fine and crumbly. Add the egg and water and process for a further 15 seconds, or until the mixture comes together. Turn the dough out onto a lightly floured surface and gather together into a smooth ball. Cover with plastic wrap and refrigerate for 30 minutes. Preheat the oven to hot 210°C (415°F/Gas 6–7).
2. Roll the pastry out very thinly to line thirty 5 cm (2 inch) patty tins. Prick lightly and bake for 8–9 minutes, or until golden. Allow to cool in tins.
3. Fill the shells with pesto, sliced sun-dried tomatoes and olives; tapenade, hard-boiled quail eggs and parsley; or cream cheese, chives, salmon and cucumber.

*Tartlets from left: Tapenade, quail eggs and parsley; Pesto, sun-dried tomato and black olive; Cream cheese, chives, salmon and cucumber*

# Mini Crab and Lime Quiches

*Preparation time:*
  15 minutes
*Total cooking time:*
  20 minutes
*Makes 18*

2 sheets frozen puff
  pastry, thawed
2 eggs
³/4 cup (185 ml/6 fl oz)
  coconut cream
finely grated rind of
  1 small lime
2 teaspoons lime juice
200 g (6¹/2 oz) canned
  good-quality crab
  meat, drained
1 tablespoon chopped
  fresh chives
salt and white pepper

**1.** Preheat the oven to
hot 210°C (415°F/
Gas 6–7). Cut rounds
of pastry, about 8 cm
(3 inches), to line
18 patty tins.
**2.** Beat the eggs lightly
in a small bowl and
add all the remaining
ingredients. Place about
1 tablespoon filling in
each pastry case.
**3.** Bake for 20 minutes,
or until golden.
Quiches will rise during
cooking then deflate
slightly. Serve warm or
at room temperature.

# Smoked Salmon and Leek Flans

*Preparation time:*
  20 minutes + chilling
*Total cooking time:*
  40 minutes
*Makes 6*

3 sheets frozen puff
  pastry, thawed
2 tablespoons sesame
  seeds
1 tablespoon olive oil
1 small leek, finely
  chopped
60 g (2 oz) smoked
  salmon, chopped
2 eggs
¹/4 cup (60 ml/2 fl oz)
  crème fraîche
¹/4 cup (60 ml/2 fl oz)
  cream
2 tablespoons grated
  Parmesan cheese
1 tablespoon chopped
  fresh basil
ground black pepper

**1.** Preheat the oven to
moderately hot 200°C
(400°F/Gas 6). Lightly
grease six 10 cm
(4 inch) flan tins with
melted butter or oil.
Sprinkle the pastry
sheets with sesame
seeds and, using a
rolling pin, gently press
the seeds into the
pastry. Cut rounds of
pastry large enough to
line the tins. Cover
with greaseproof paper.
Spread dried baking
beans or rice to the top
of the tins and chill in
the refrigerator for
10 minutes.
**2.** Bake in the oven
for 10 minutes, then
discard the paper and
beans and cook for a
further 5 minutes. If the
pastry has risen in the
middle, press it down.
Reduce the oven to
moderate 180°C
(350°F/Gas 4).
**3.** Heat the oil in a
frying pan, add the leek
and stir over low heat
for 5 minutes, or until
soft. Remove from the
heat and cool slightly.
Spread the cooked leek
evenly over the bases of
the pastries and top
with salmon.
**4.** Combine the eggs,
crème fraîche and
cream in a bowl, whisk
until smooth and stir in
the cheese, basil and
pepper. Pour gently
over the salmon and
leek. Bake for about
15–20 minutes, or until
the filling is set and
lightly browned on top.

*Mini Crab and Lime Quiches (top)*
*with Smoked Salmon and Leek Flans*

# Filo Triangles

These delicate triangles of flaking filo with their moist fillings are ideal for passing round at parties or as family nibbles.

❖ ◆ ❖ ◆ ❖ ◆

**To make the Triangles:**
Preheat the oven to moderately hot 190°C. (375°F/Gas 5). Cover 16 sheets of filo pastry with a slightly damp tea towel—work with one sheet at a time to avoid the pastry drying out. Brush a sheet of pastry with melted butter or olive oil. Lay a second sheet on top, brush and then cut lengthways into three even strips. Place a tablespoon of your choice of filling (see right) at the end of the pastry and fold up to form a triangle. Place on a lightly oiled oven tray and cover with a slightly damp tea towel while repeating with the remaining pastry and filling. Brush with oil or melted butter and bake for 15–20 minutes, or until golden brown. Makes 24.

*Triangles, from left: Three Cheese; Prawn and Crab; Spinach and Pinenut; Chicken and Basil; Curried Pumpkin*

## Three Cheese Triangles

Put 160 g (5 1/4 oz) crumbled feta, 1 cup (250 g/8 oz) ricotta and 1 cup (90 g/3 oz) grated Cheddar cheese in a bowl. Add 4 tablespoons finely chopped parsley, 1–2 cloves finely chopped garlic, freshly ground black pepper, to taste, and 1 lightly beaten egg. Stir until well combined.

## Prawn and Crab Triangles

Melt 30 g (1 oz) butter in a small saucepan; add 3 finely chopped spring onions and cook for 2 minutes until softened. Stir in 1 tablespoon plain flour then stir in 1/2 cup (125 ml/4 fl oz) milk. Stir until thickened and remove from the heat, then add 1 tablespoon each of cream and lemon juice and 3 tablespoons finely chopped parsley. Using your hands, squeeze dry 170 g (5 1/2 oz) canned white meat crab and 200 g (6 1/2 oz) canned prawns. Mix with the sauce.

## Spinach and Pinenut Triangles

Cover 250 g (8 oz) spinach leaves with boiling water and leave to soften. Squeeze out all the liquid and chop finely. Place in a bowl with 2 tablespoons lightly toasted pinenuts, 1 teaspoon nutmeg, 2 finely chopped spring onions, 1–2 cloves crushed garlic, 125 g (4 oz) each crumbled feta and ricotta cheeses and 1 lightly beaten egg. Stir to combine.

## Chicken and Basil Triangles

Heat 1 tablespoon olive oil in a small frying pan; add 1 small finely chopped red onion and cook for 2 minutes, until softened. Remove from the heat and stir in 1 small, chopped, cooked chicken breast, 2 teaspoons seeded mustard, 6 finely chopped sun-dried tomatoes, 125 g (4 oz) ricotta, 1/2 cup (30 g/1 oz) chopped basil and 60 g (2 oz) each grated Parmesan and Cheddar. Stir until well combined.

## Curried Pumpkin Triangles

Heat 30 g (1 oz) butter in a small frying pan, add 4 finely chopped spring onions and cook for 2 minutes, or until the onions are softened. Stir in 2 tablespoons plain flour and 1 teaspoon curry powder and cook for a further 2 minutes. Place in a bowl, together with 1 cup (250 g/8 oz) cooked and mashed pumpkin (this will be about 500 g/1 lb uncooked pumpkin), 1 beaten egg, 125 g (4 oz) ricotta cheese and 1/2 cup (60 g/2 oz) grated Parmesan. Stir until well combined.

## Caviar Puffs

*Preparation time:*
  1 hour
*Total cooking time:*
  25 minutes
*Makes 30*

*1 quantity choux pastry
(page 3)*

### Filling
*6 hard-boiled eggs
salt and freshly ground
  black pepper
2 tablespoons finely
  grated onion
2 tablespoons finely
  chopped chives
1/4 cup (60 g/2 oz)
  mayonnaise*

### Topping
*sour cream
45 g (1 1/4 oz) jar black
  or red caviar*

**1.** Preheat the oven to
moderately hot 200°C
(400°F/Gas 6). Using
2 teaspoons, spoon
30 balls of choux onto
a lightly oiled tray,
allowing room for
rising. Bake for
20 minutes, then reduce
the oven to moderate
180°C (350°F/Gas 4)
and bake for a further
5 minutes, or until
golden and puffed.
Pierce the sides of the
puffs to allow the
steam to escape. Leave
to cool on a wire rack.

Cut off the tops of the
choux puffs.
**2. To make Filling:** Peel
and mash the eggs; add
salt, pepper, onion,
chives and mayonnaise.
Just before serving, fill
each puff with a
teaspoon of filling;
replace the lid and top
with a dollop of sour
cream and caviar.

## Pumpkin Quiches

*Preparation time:*
  30 minutes +
  refrigeration
*Total cooking time:*
  1 hour 30 minutes
*Makes 8*

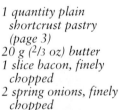

*1 quantity plain
  shortcrust pastry
  (page 3)
20 g (2/3 oz) butter
1 slice bacon, finely
  chopped
2 spring onions, finely
  chopped
1–2 cloves garlic,
  crushed
1 cup (250 g/8 oz)
  cooked and mashed
  pumpkin (500 g raw)
2 eggs, lightly beaten
2/3 cup (170 ml/
  5 1/2 fl oz) cream
3 tablespoons chopped
  fresh parsley
1/2 teaspoon nutmeg
freshly ground black
  pepper*

**1.** Preheat the oven to
moderately hot 190°C
(375°F/Gas 5). Roll out
the pastry between
2 sheets of baking
paper. Line eight 10 cm
(4 inch) loose-based
fluted flan tins with the
pastry and refrigerate
for 20 minutes. Cover
each tin with a square
of baking paper and fill
with baking beans or
rice. Place the tins on a
baking tray and bake
blind for 10 minutes,
remove the paper and
beans and return to the
oven for 2–3 minutes to
dry out. Leave to cool.
**2.** Heat the butter in a
saucepan. Cook the
bacon, spring onions
and garlic for about
3 minutes. Transfer the
mixture to a large
mixing bowl and stir in
the pumpkin, eggs,
cream, parsley, nutmeg
and pepper.
**3.** Spoon the filling into
the prepared pastry
cases. Bake for 20
minutes, or until the
filling is lightly golden.
Serve immediately.

**Note:** Peel and cut the
pumpkin into 5 cm
(2 inch) cubes, brush
with a little oil, then
roast for 1 hour at
180°C (350°F/Gas 4),
or until cooked. Cool
before mashing.

*Caviar Puffs (top) with Pumpkin Quiches*

## Sweet Onion and Feta Tarts

*Preparation time:*
  15 minutes + chilling
*Total cooking time:*
  45 minutes
*Serves 6*

1 cup (125 g/4 oz) plain
  flour
1/4 teaspoon salt
110 g (32/3 oz) butter,
  chopped
1 tablespoon bottled
  green peppercorns,
  drained
1 egg yolk
1 teaspoon Dijon
  mustard
2 teaspoons water

**Sweet Onion Filling**
2 tablespoons olive oil
3 medium onions,
  sliced
1 clove garlic, sliced
2 teaspoons sugar
2 tablespoons Balsamic
  vinegar
3 tablespoons raisins
2 teaspoons olive paste
75 g (21/2 oz) feta
  cheese

**1.** Lightly grease six
10 cm shallow loose-
based tart tins.
**2.** Sift the flour and salt
into a large bowl and
rub in the butter. Crush
the peppercorns in a
mortar and pestle or
with the flat side of a
knife. Make a well in

the centre of the flour
and butter mixture and
add the combined
peppercorns, egg yolk,
mustard and enough
water to make the
ingredients just cling
together and form a
dough. Cover with
plastic wrap and
refrigerate for about
20 minutes. Preheat the
oven to moderately hot
200°C (400°F/Gas 6).
**3.** Divide the dough
into six equal portions
and press into the bases
and sides of the tins.
Prick well with a fork
and bake for 15
minutes or until golden.
**4. To make Sweet
Onion Filling**: Heat the
olive oil in a heavy-
based pan. Add the
onions and garlic and
cook, covered, over
low heat for about
30 minutes, or until the
onions are very soft and
beginning to brown.
Increase the heat to
moderate, add the sugar
and vinegar and cook,
stirring, until most of
the liquid has
evaporated and the
onion mixture is glossy.
Stir in the raisins.
**5.** Spread a little olive
paste over the base of
each pastry case. Spoon
over the onion mixture
and crumble the feta on
top. These tarts can be
served warm or at room
temperature.

## Prawn and Scallop Vol au Vents

*Preparation time:*
  25 minutes
*Total cooking time:*
  20 minutes
*Makes 12*

1 cup (250 ml/8 fl oz)
  fish stock
1 cup (250 ml/8 fl oz)
  white wine
250 g (8 oz) scallops
250 g (8 oz) peeled
  raw prawns
60 g (2 oz) butter
4 spring onions,
  chopped
1 slice bacon, chopped
1/4 cup (30 g/1 oz) plain
  flour
1/2 cup (125 ml/4 fl oz)
  cream
1 teaspoon lemon juice
salt and black pepper
1/2 cup (30 g/1 oz)
  finely chopped parsley
12 x 6 cm ready-made
  vol au vent cases

**1.** Heat the stock and
wine in a pan until
simmering. Add the
scallops and cook
gently for 2–3 minutes.
Remove to a plate with
a slotted spoon, cool
and chop. Repeat with
the prawns. Reserve
1 cup (250 ml/8 fl oz)
of the liquid.
Refrigerate the seafood
while making the sauce.
Preheat the oven to

*Sweet Onion and Feta Tarts (top) with Prawn and Scallop Vol au Vents*

160°C (315°F/Gas 2–3).
**2.** Melt the butter in a pan. Add the onions and bacon and cook over medium heat for 3 minutes, until cooked but not browned; add the flour and cook for 2 minutes. Add the reserved liquid and stir until thickened. Stir in the cream, juice, salt, pepper and parsley, saving some to garnish.

**3.** Heat the vol au vent cases for 5 minutes. Reheat the sauce, stir in the seafood and warm through. Divide among the cases, garnish with parsley and serve.

53

1  *Process the flour, salt and butter until crumbly, then add the sesame seeds.*

2  *An easy way to trim away excess pastry is to use a rolling pin.*

# Warm Duck And Coriander Tarts

*Preparation time:*
  35 minutes + chilling
*Total cooking time:*
  20 minutes
*Makes 8*

1<sup>1</sup>/2 cups (185 g/6 oz)
  plain flour
<sup>1</sup>/2 teaspoon salt
125 g (4 oz) chilled
  butter, chopped
3 tablespoons sesame
  seeds
2 tablespoons iced
  water

**Filling**
1 large Chinese roasted
  duck
2 tablespoons orange
  marmalade
1 tablespoon kecap
  manis
1 tablespoon lime juice
2 teaspoons sesame oil
1 tablespoon grated
  fresh ginger
5 finely sliced green
  spring onions
2 tablespoons chopped
  fresh coriander, plus
  extra sprigs to garnish

1. Process the flour, salt and butter for 10–15 seconds, or until fine and crumbly. Add the sesame seeds and water and process for a further 10–15 seconds, or until the mixture just comes together. Turn the dough out onto a lightly floured surface and gather together to form a smooth ball.
2. Preheat the oven to hot 210°C (415°F, Gas 6–7). Divide the dough into 8 portions. Roll out thinly to line eight 9 cm (3<sup>1</sup>/2 inch) tart tins and prick the bases lightly. Bake the pastry cases for 15 minutes, or until golden brown, and then refrigerate for about 20 minutes.
3. **To make Filling:** Remove the duck meat from the bones and shred the meat. Put the marmalade in a pan and stir until smooth. Add the remaining ingredients, including the shredded duck, and mix well. Heat until warmed through.
4. Arrange the warm pastry shells on serving plates and add the warm filling. Garnish with coriander and serve immediately as a starter or light lunch.

**Note:** The skin from the duck may also be used in the filling, however all visible fat should be removed. Kecap manis is an Indonesian soy sauce, available in Asian supermarkets.

*Warm Duck and Coriander Tart*

3  Remove the duck meat from the bones and shred.

4  Stir the marmalade over heat until smooth; add the remaining ingredients.

55

# Sausage Rolls

These traditional favourites can be spiced up to suit any occasion. Try some new variations on an old and trusted theme.

## Basic Recipe

Preheat the oven to 200°C (400°F/Gas 6). Cut 3 sheets of ready-rolled puff or flaky pastry in half and brush the edges with beaten egg. Divide your choice of filling (see right) into 6 even portions. Pipe or spoon filling down the centre of each piece of pastry, then brush the edge with egg. Fold the pastry over the filling and overlap the edges, placing the join underneath. Brush the rolls with egg, then cut into short pieces. Cut 2 small slashes on top of each roll and place on a lightly greased baking tray. Bake for 15 minutes, then reduce the oven to moderate 180°C (350°F/Gas 4) and bake for a further 15 minutes, or until the rolls are puffed and golden. Makes 36.

## Herbed Sausage Filling

Put 750 g (1 lb 8 oz) sausage mince, 1 finely chopped onion, 1 clove crushed garlic, 1 cup (90 g/3 oz) fresh breadcrumbs, 1 lightly beaten egg, 1/2 cup (30 g/1 oz) chopped parsley, 3 tablespoons chopped thyme and 1/2 teaspoon each ground sage, nutmeg, black pepper and cloves in a large bowl and mix together well.

## Curried Pork and Veal Filling

Soak 3 dried Chinese mushrooms in hot water for 30 minutes; squeeze dry and chop finely. Sauté 4 finely chopped spring onions, 1–2 cloves garlic, 1 finely chopped small red chilli and 2–3 teaspoons curry powder in 1 tablespoon oil. Transfer to a large bowl and add 750 g (1 lb 8 oz) pork and veal mince, the dried mushrooms, 1 cup (90 g/3 oz) fresh breadcrumbs, 1 lightly beaten egg, 3 tablespoons chopped coriander and 1 tablespoon each soy and oyster sauce. Stir until well combined.

*Sausage Rolls from left: Herbed Sausage; Curried Pork and Veal; Spicy Lamb; Saucy Beef; Chutney Chicken*

## Spicy Lamb Filling

In a bowl, mix 750 g (1 lb 8 oz) lamb mince, 1 cup (90 g/3 oz) fresh breadcrumbs, 1 small grated onion, 1 tablespoon soy sauce, 2 teaspoons each of grated fresh ginger and soft brown sugar, 1 teaspoon ground coriander, 1/2 teaspoon each of ground cumin and sambal oelek. Lightly sprinkle the pastry rolls with poppy seeds after glazing and before baking.

## Saucy Beef Filling

Sauté 1 finely chopped onion and 1–2 cloves garlic in 20 g (2/3 oz) butter until the onion is softened. In a large bowl mix together 750 g (1 lb 8 oz) lean mince, the sautéed onion and garlic, 3 tablespoons finely chopped parsley, 3 tablespoons plain flour, 3 tablespoons tomato sauce, 1 tablespoon each of Worcestershire and soy sauces and 2 teaspoons ground allspice until well combined.

## Chutney Chicken Filling

In a bowl, mix together 750 g (1 lb 8 oz) chicken mince, 4 finely chopped spring onions, 1 cup (90 g/3 oz) fresh breadcrumbs, 1 finely grated carrot, 2 tablespoons fruit chutney, 1 tablespoon each of sweet chilli sauce and grated fresh ginger until well combined. Once the rolls have been filled and cut, lightly sprinkle the pastry with sesame seeds after glazing and before baking.

## Spinach and Feta Pies

*Preparation time:*
  30 minutes + chilling
*Total cooking time:*
  30 minutes
*Makes 12*

*500 g (1 lb) English*
  *spinach*
*100 g feta cheese,*
  *crumbled*
*1 tablespoon olive oil*
*1 small red onion,*
  *finely chopped*
*2 spring onions, finely*
  *chopped*
*1/2 red capsicum, finely*
  *chopped*
*1–2 cloves garlic,*
  *crushed*
*1/2 teaspoon dried basil*
*1 tablespoon cream*
*1 quantity rough puff*
  *pastry (page 4)*
*1 egg, lightly beaten*

**1.** Grease a baking tray with melted butter or oil. Wash and remove the stalks from the spinach. Put the wet leaves in a large pan, cover and cook over low heat for 2 minutes, or until wilted. Drain, cool, squeeze the leaves dry with your hands and roughly chop. Place in a large bowl with the feta and set aside.
**2.** In a frying pan, heat the oil; add the onion, spring onion, capsicum, garlic and basil. Cook, stirring, over medium heat for 5 minutes, or until cooked. Stir in the cream and then add to the spinach and feta mixture while hot. Stir to thoroughly combine.
**3.** For ease of handling, roll out half the pastry at a time, keeping the other half chilled. Cut twelve 8 cm (3 inch) pastry rounds using a plain cutter. Brush each with beaten egg around the outside edge. Place a tablespoon of the spinach filling onto each pastry round.
**4.** Roll out the remaining pastry and cut another 12 rounds. Place these over the filled pastry bases, pressing gently to seal. Make a small incision in the top of each pastry to allow steam to escape during cooking. With the back end of a knife make small indentations at regular intervals around the outside edge of each pie. This helps the pastry to rise and form flakes. Place on the baking tray. Cover the pies and refrigerate for at least 20 minutes. Meanwhile, preheat the oven to hot 210°C (415°F/Gas 6–7). Bake for 20 minutes, or until puffed and golden. Serve at once.

## Chicken Curry Pasties

*Preparation time:*
  30 minutes
*Cooking time:*
  30 minutes
*Makes 20*

*2 tablespoons oil*
*1 small onion, finely*
  *chopped*
*1 clove garlic, crushed*
*2 teaspoons curry*
  *powder*
*1 potato, finely*
  *chopped*
*200 g (6 1/2 oz) chicken*
  *mince*
*1/3 cup (60 g/2 oz)*
  *frozen peas*
*1 tablespoon finely*
  *chopped fresh parsley*
*5 sheets ready-rolled*
  *puff pastry*
*1 egg, lightly beaten*

**1.** Preheat the oven to moderate 180°C (350°F/Gas 4). Line an oven tray with foil. Heat the oil in a heavy-based frying pan. Add the onion and garlic and cook over medium heat for 2 minutes, or until the onion is soft. Add the curry powder and cook, stirring, for 1 minute. Add the potato, stir to combine, cover and cook for a few minutes until it begins to soften.
**2.** Add the chicken

# Mini Quiche Lorraines

*Preparation time:*
20 minutes
*Total cooking time:*
25 minutes
*Makes 24*

1 quantity plain
  shortcrust pastry
  (page 3)
50 g (1²/3 oz) Gruyère
  cheese, cut into
  thin strips
1 tablespoon butter
2 slices bacon, finely
  chopped
1 onion, finely chopped
2 eggs
³/4 cup (185 ml/6 fl oz)
  cream
¹/2 teaspoon nutmeg
freshly ground black
  pepper
chive tips, to decorate

**1.** Preheat the oven to
moderately hot 190°C
(375°F/Gas 5). Roll the
pastry between two
sheets of baking paper.
Using a plain cutter, cut
rounds of pastry to fit
deep patty tins. Divide
the cheese strips evenly
over the pastry bases.
Place the pastries on a
baking tray, cover with
plastic wrap and
refrigerate while
making the filling.

**2.** Heat the butter in a
small pan and cook the
bacon and onion for
2–3 minutes until
tender. Drain on paper
towels. When cool,
divide the mixture
evenly among the
pastries. Whisk the
eggs in a bowl with the
cream, nutmeg and
pepper. Pour carefully
into the pastry shells.
**3.** Place 2–3 chive tips
on top of each quiche
to decorate. Bake for
20 minutes, or until
lightly browned and
set. Serve hot or warm.

# Goats Cheese and Apple Tarts

*Preparation time:*
10 minutes
*Total cooking time:*
20 minutes
*Makes 4*

1 sheet frozen puff
  pastry
155 g (5 oz) fresh goats
  cheese, sliced
2 granny smith apples,
  unpeeled
1 tablespoon extra
  virgin olive oil
2 teaspoons chopped
  fresh lemon thyme
salt and freshly ground
  black pepper

**1.** Preheat the oven to
hot 210°C (415°F/
Gas 6–7). While the
pastry is still frozen, cut
it into four squares and
place apart on a lightly
greased oven tray. Set
aside for a few minutes
to thaw and then lay
the cheese over the
pastry, leaving a 2 cm
(³/4 inch) border.
**2.** Core the apples and
slice thinly. Interleave
the slices over the
pastry, making sure
the cheese is covered
completely. Brush the
apples liberally with oil
and sprinkle with
lemon thyme and a
little salt and pepper
to taste.
**3.** Bake the tarts for
20 minutes, or until
the pastry is cooked
through and golden
brown at the edges.
Tarts are best served
immediately.

**Note:** An ideal salad to
serve with these tarts is
a combination of
rocket, radicchio and
butter lettuce leaves
plus a few broken
walnut halves, all
tossed gently with a
vinaigrette dressing.

---

*Mini Quiche Lorraines (top)
with Goats Cheese and Apple Tarts*

# Index